original
love

original
love

p o e m s

molly
peacock

w. w. norton & company new york • london

The text of this book is composed in Linotype Waldbaum
with the display set in Linotype Waldbaum
Composition and manufacturing by Maple-Vail
Book Manufacturing Group.
Book design by Chris Welch

Library of Congress Cataloging-in-Publication Data

Peacock, Molly, 1947–
Original love : poems / Molly Peacock.
p.   cm.
1. Love poetry.   I. Title.
PS3566.E15075   1995
811'.54—dc20   94-27504

ISBN 0-393-03741-X

W. W. Norton & Company, Inc., 500 Fifth Avenue, New York, N.Y. 10110
W. W. Norton & Company Ltd., 10 Coptic Street, London WC1A 1PU

1 2 3 4 5 6 7 8 9 0

for Michael Groden

contents

acknowledgments

The following poems, perhaps in earlier versions, appeared originally in these magazines or anthologies:

The New Republic: "The Hunt," "Portrayal"
The Nation: "Floral Conversation"
Ms.: "The Fare," "Seeing a Basket of Lobelia
   the Color of a Bathrobe"
The Paris Review: "Why I Am Not a Buddhist,"
   "Waking Up," "The Rule," "I Consider the
   Possibility," "Have You Ever Faked an Orgasm?"
   "The Return," "My College Sex Group"
Boulevard: "Greeting Card Verse,"
   "The Explanation" (under the title "The Site")
Ploughshares: "Forgiveness," "Yes," "No"
The Southwest Review: "Prairie Prayer"
Tangled Vines: "Housecleaning"
Hampden-Sydney Poetry Review: "Interrupted Elegy"
   (under the title "Cancelled Elegy")

Crosscurrents: "In a Long Line of Horses"
The Northern Sentinel: "Love Wall," "Unseen"
Lips: "Instructions to Miss Muffet," "Vogue Vista"
The Formalist: "Happy Birthday," "The Guilt"
Verse: "Religious Instruction," "Subway Vespers"
American Letters and Commentary: "The Gown"
Lilt: "Upbringing"
Sojourner: "Dogged Persistence," "The Raptor"

"The Wheel" appeared as a broadside from
    Salmon Run Press.

My deepest thanks and love to Phillis Levin, William Louis-Dreyfus, and Georgianna Orsini for their insight into these poems as they were being written.

My love and thanks as well to Nita Buchanan, Barbara Feldon, Katie Kinsky, Elise Paschen, Joan Stein, and Anne West for many kindnesses which helped me better understand the themes of *Original Love*.

And to Richard Burgin, Lynn Emmanuel, Michael Fried, Richard Howard, Lisi Schoenbach, and Carol Houck Smith, all of whom have had faith and new ideas for my work, my gratitude.

The Stadler Center for Poetry at Bucknell University, Friends Seminary, the National Endowment for the Arts, and the New York Foundation for the Arts provided safe harbors for the writing of these poems.

Why I Am Not a Buddhist

I love desire, the state of want and thought
of how to get; building a kingdom in a soul
requires desire. I love the things I've sought—
you in your beltless bathrobe, tongues of cash that loll
from my billfold—and love what I want: clothes,
houses, redemption. Can a new mauve suit
equal God? Oh no, desire is ranked. To lose
a loved pen is not like losing faith. Acute
desire for nut gateau is driven out by death,
but the cake on its plate has meaning,
even when love is endangered and nothing matters.
For my mother, health; for my sister, bereft,
wholeness. But why is desire suffering?
Because want leaves a world in tatters?
How else but in tatters should a world be?
A columned porch set high above a lake.
Here, take my money. A loved face in agony,
the spirit gone. Here, use my rags of love.

part I

first
love

Life Study

Take a blank page   'v
a line to the mid'   .
This is perspec'
In life that lir   or
to abrade. V   to draw
3-dimensi   ʒe?
Because healinɡ   ıto day.
Fully lighted, kindnε.   to repay
some of the abuse. Now faι   ιre appealing
and complex, their angles jumping into relief.
Now real rain enlivens vistas from the depths
of hopes deserted at too young an age. Trauma
redistributes its colors, old drama quelled
to tables laid for meals, now actually eaten.
You could say I've whitewashed my youth, since light
from the end of the tunnel washes back through:
as I draw I see not what I stumbled through,
but each illumined site.

The Wheel

Because of your nose, like a leaf blade
turned outward; because of the veins, also
leaflike, but stronger, surging up your forearms;
because of the moles spotting your arms
and neck and face like a long mottled animal;
because of the thrillingly perfect grades you made;
because no other girl had you (and I felt
you might want to be had) and beyond this felt
you would not refuse me, I made my play
at Junior Carnival, and threw myself at you
as if I'd done it a thousand times before
(and of course I had—I'd thrown myself away
on my parents' refusals), as if I knew
for certain you'd receive me at the door

of the side gymnasium, flattered, shy,
talking quickly back to me, leaning your shoulder
against the threshhold, me leaning closer,
smelling your laundered shirt, you not questioning why
I had chosen you, the one gripping the math folder,
gently accepting my self-exposure
(so needing acceptance yourself); because
of all this I ask you twenty-five years later
to be my husband and you ask me
to be your wife, our first wishes
confirmed at last as our best, spun out, original,
as if our lives were a novel ending (it really
makes sense you left math for literature) with kisses,
and from the games in the dim gymnasium, applause
as the frozen wheel of fortune thaws.

So What If I Am in Love

The penguin sweatshirt I slept in smelled both
of him and time, if time has odor, worn,
softened as skin asleep, blurred as the breath

beneath the faded lines of a bird born
on a shirt, not in a nest. Completely torn
between delight and the imagined wrath,

the sheer disaster of my life torn down if
the shirt were ever found, I accepted
his gift and got on the subway with

my makeup, my papers, my underwear
all stuffed in the bag where it lay, given,
given to me! in my lap in the glare

of trainlight. "Beware," the panic-driven
self says, "No, no you can't," even
at the cost of your growth. But I left it there.

When the doors opened, I leapt out, turned around,
saw it on the seat as the train rushed past,
screaming "No!" so loud a man turned around.

"I left a gift on the train," I said, aghast.
"At least it wasn't cash," he said while the past,
worn, softened, blurred as the lines of the bird,

a comic little figure in the arctic waste
of the white shirt, unfroze inside me, stirred
by the loss and relieved by what I dared

at last to feel. I wobbled home as if
tossed from floe to floe of a broken jam,
from if, to am, to so what if I am.

My College Sex Group

All my girlfriends were talking about sex
and the vibrators they ordered from Eve's
Garden which came with genital portraits
of twelve different girls. All my friends' needs
swirled around me while their conversations
about positions crescendoed and they waved
their vibrators—black rubber things. Saved
by volubility I looked at the relations
of labia to clitori—look, there was one
like mine, labia like chicken wattles
below a hooded clitoris. "Friends!
of these twelve genital portraits, which
are you?" I couldn't ask them. Happy
to have found a picture of one like me:
the portrait held the hair all back and popped
the clitoris out like a snapdragon
above the dark vaginal stem.
Oh God, it was me! (And another, I stopped,
there were others like us, throughout the world.)
When my order for the vibrator was filled,
I'd get my own portrait. I'd show it to the next boy
before I got undressed: "Here's what you're getting."
And I'm not alone, or ugly, if that's what you're thinking.

Have You Ever Faked an Orgasm?

When I get nervous, it's so hard not to.
When I'm expected to come in something
other than my ordinary way, to
take pleasure in the new way, lost, not knowing

how to drive it back to sureness . . . where are
the thousand thousand flowers I always pass,
the violet flannel, then the sharpness?
I can't, I can't . . . extinguish the star

in a burst. It goes on glowing. Your head
between my legs so long. Do you really
want to be there? I whimper as though . . .
then get mad. I could smash your valiant head.

"You didn't come, did you?" Naturally, you know.
Although I try to lie, the truth escapes me
almost like an orgasm itself. Then the "No"
that should crack a world, but doesn't, slips free.

Panties and the Buddha

Frantic to finish, frantic not to forget
details for a thousand deadlines,
"Clean underpants!" I think in the shower,
get out, drag a plastic tub, and string a line
under the tropic showerhead, grabbing clothespins,
hauling soap and dirty silk panties back
behind the curtain with me, still wed
to ALL THINGS NOW! (Poor Buddha, there's an ax
in your back.) *Make of yourself a lightness*,
Buddha says. Loofahs, gels, rinses and shampoos:
timing the hair rinse to rinsing the pants
—clip each by its crotch, lace dripping.

I won't know I have a body until you,
darling, imagine this lingerie on me as I
excuse myself to the ladies' room stall
of this restaurant in a foreign city
to lean my forehead on the marble, all
items on my lists crossed out, and the ax
I put in the Buddha's back starts slipping out
as I hike up a silk jungle print on my ass,
glad to remember I have one, as you
always remind me how glad you are to feel
this silk beneath the plain wool of my slacks.

The Return

When I open my legs to let you seek,
seek inside me, seeking more, I think
"What are you looking for?" and feel it will
be hid from me, whatever it is, still
or rapidly moving beyond my frequency.
Then I declare you a mystery
and stop myself from moving and hold still
until you can find your orgasm. Peak
is partly what you look for, and the brink
you love to come to and return to must
be part of it, too, thrust, build, the trust
that brings me, surprised, to a brink of my own . . .
I must be blind to something of my own
you recognize and look for. A diamond
speaks in a way through its beams, though it's dumb
to the brilliance it reflects. A gem at the back
of the cave must tell you, "Yes, you can go back."

Love Wall

Because you know you are not me and
I know I am not you, I love you and
am content among my pillows, prints, and
flowers in my room next to your room. The bond
of love that binds our days without a magic wand
to blur the boundaries between my soft land
and your crisp room's equipment, awards, and
lean black frames removes the command
to merge, merge, and die. My mother's hand
snakes around the banister and gropes. I shut
the door. *But you are me*, it cries, *I am you, cut
off from your own wrist!* Quick I look down: two hands,
—both mine, at my arms' ends—proof the command
is disobeyed. I think of leashing her hand
to keep it as a pet, but leave my door shut,
as if telling my neighbor's cat to go home. And
you who are not me work in your room, blandly
remaining separate, our wall our ampersand.

Waking Up

I try to keep the promises I make
—for each one broken breaks the world—and seem
inhuman: no crack, no fissure, no mistake.

Control of life is fear for fear's own sake.
A teacup soldered or a split of silk reseamed:
fixing them, I keep the promises I make.

To lower the pressure, I lower the stakes;
the weight of covenants can make me scream
inhuman howls at my human mistakes,

a perfectionist caught in an earthquake.
I lower the stakes and whimper in my dreams
a prayer for a whole life (a promise *kept*) to make

sense. How childish I feel when I remake
childhood's dream: all things delivered in a stream
of consistency—no crack, no fissure, no mistake,

all done when planned. But swans arrive at their lake
each year, called home by the angle of sunbeams.
Surrender to nature's perfection means

to know one's nature, no mistake. Sometimes it seems
a life's asleep beneath my frenzy, and I wake
from a promise of youth that I no longer make.

The Scare

When the nervous excitement in his voice
spreads through the phone like watercolor on
a wet page and first I brighten, then hoist
myself up in bed and turn the light on,
unaccountably asking him what's wrong
(is something offcolor in his brilliance?)
he says that he lifted something up wrong,
felt a pull behind his rib, poked in the dense
tissue beneath it, thinking he found a lump
not quite like the lump from his last cancer,
then he really knew, it could just be a bump
from the weight strain, this anxiety recurs
whenever . . . "Of course it recurs, you idiot,
we've just gotten married!" I don't say.

Images of helping him die spill, like aquatint,
across the sheets. "Not now," I don't pray,
and the dry sheets of my bed feel wet with
the painted images of the hospital bed,
the drip of the IV, radiation, chemotherapy,
the cancer spread, the bedspread wet with
—I've upset a glass of water. "Now listen
I love you, please get on the plane, your rib
will heal, then we'll feel for the lump." Glisten
of adrenalized halo . . . A shining nib,
my voice draws counterlines on his bright fast
voice strokes. How will I ever keep it up?
Don't crawl into prayer posture yet. *Hang up.*
Shut down. Dry off. You've got to last.

Marathon Song

I love you at the finish line.
I love you wishing you had run.
I love you saying you will next time.
I love you at the marathon.

We stand here on a big flat rock
on which we've placed a big fat book
so we can get a good high look
at all the runners near the clock.

I love you in repressed fear,
expressed hope, panic, fervor,
and hypocritical nonchalance here,
perched on *The Reincarnation Reader*,

all about life after death. You say, *"Can
you see?"* I can see just fine when
our heels grind up the past and future.
I love your even-tempered nature.

I love it that only a minor
injury kept you from the stepped-up
training a long-term cancer survivor
must do—now you're all prepped

to run for your life again next year.
I love you in mortal fear
and when the center goes dark.
I love you on a book in Central Park.

The Purr

As you stand still in the hall thinking what
to do next and I approach you from behind,
I think behind must be best: your naked
rump scalloped beneath the plumb

line of your spine's furred tree. But
as I catch the concentration in the kind
angling of your head toward the cats and tread
catlike myself behind you, your scrotum

hung like an oriole's nest, I cut
beneath your outstretched arm and find
I'm hungry for your face instead,
hungry for my future. The mysterious thrum

that science can't yet explain awakes a hum
in me, the sound something numb come alive makes.

Lullaby

Big as a down duvet the night
pulls the close Ontario sky
over the naked earth. Here we lie
gossiping in a circle of light

under our own big comforter
buried nude as b   "
to grow your hya
Far above, the co

on the comforter th
is to real earth. Star
above; down here ou   ..retlies
on flannel around us. Night turns

to surround the planet. Earth settles
real hyacinths in place. You yield,
turning like night's face to settle
on me, chest on breasts, your field.

Little Miracle

No use getting hysterical.
The important part is: we're here.
Our lives are a little miracle.

My hummingbird-hearted schedule
beats its shiny frenzy, day into year.
No use getting hysterical—

it's always like that. The oracle
a human voice could be is shrunk by fear.
Our lives are a little miracle

—we must remind ourselves—whimsical,
and lyrical, large and slow and clear.
(So no use getting hysterical!)

All words other than *I love you* are clerical,
dispensable, and replaceable, my dear.
Our inner lives are a miracle.

They beat their essence in the coracle
our ribs provide, the watertight boat we steer
through others' acid, hysterical
demands. Ours is the miracle: *we're here.*

Blush Blessing

My luxury is in the ordinary when
I step into a crowd of people who grin
at the bus driver as they drop in the exact
change they've had time to remember. They're not in
trouble, it seems, or in chemo, in X ray, in pain; in fact
it seems they're in their own heads, not worrying
whether they or those they love will die or why
things are the way they are. I join their ring,
pearled; their world, adored; and cry their cry
of mild annoyance at the tiny imperfections
we all have time to notice. This attractive
woman on the bus for instance, in a red concoction
of cape and boots below her black hair—just to *live*
to note this final, off detail!—has put

pink! the wrong color for her outfit, on her lips.
How annoying, her slightly misshaded choice.
(What she needs is a creamy carmine red
the color of her cape.) Darling, when this bus
delivers me home to our clean apartment to be fed
the meal over which I had the time to fuss,
let me make a little fuss about something
insignificant, the malfunction of some silly
piece of hardware, or the wrong hair coloring,
or details for our party, before we pile willy-
nilly into bed with chocolate and video and prepare
to make love. The way a radiator hiss
makes a perfect indoor snowy silence hush,
the flicker of a bother trues the world in which we kiss.

part *II*

mother
love

The Spider Heart

Sleeping with my husband in my mother's bed
the night she died, I expected the tree—
the one that Emerson said grew tall and wide
after his father died—but woke up instead
with a spider wedged in my rib cage, scrambling.
It was crablike, black, and horizontal,
like a squat tree on its side. One set of legs
was the roots thrashing against my ribs; the other
was short energetic branches without leaves.
It was a stunted winter tree. It was a winter night.
I lay cold and frightened under my mother's quilt,
but I covered up my husband instead,
lying there, a bit corpselike from exhaustion,
but breathing, while she was being driven
to her hometown, where her plot was.

Death opens the plot of a life: all during
the hideous book of her illness I thought
she had a sad, terrible life, but in her bed
the spider's clawing grew so sharp I had
to count to calm myself down, and so I gave
each year of her life a number, expecting
bad after bad year, but adding up the worst
at ten, a seventh of her life—no worse
than anyone's! Why had I misjudged the pain?
The same ten years quartered my life, doubling
the dose of her daily absences, the helpless
fights with her husband when she returned,
and my constant, childish fear we would all die
from her going away. Then I knew
the terrible scrambling was my own survival.
And I slept, despite the racket in my rib cage,
startling to the alarm on my husband's watch,
heart pounding from waking without enough sleep.

It was time to get going, but I lay there.
I wasn't going to have Ralph Waldo
Emerson's tree. The huge arachnid lay there.
I decided to describe it to my husband
to make it smaller; then I could get up
and we could drive out to my mother's town.
To do this, I looked hard behind my ribs
and the spider changed under my watching eye,
its thorax elongating, its legs flexing
ballerinalike, its color fading
to the translucency of dancer's tights, silvery
as birchbark—one set of legs rootlike,
whiter, one set branchlike, darker, though still
horizontal. As we got out of bed
I had two limbs of a thought at once:
You haven't seen the end of that spider
came first; then the other,
How will you set the birchtree upright?

Seeing a Basket of Lobelia the Color
of a Bathrobe

in the galley of a barge

At that time I read a book about a girl prone
to perfection: her mother had just died.
As she prepared her first supper, she tried
to peel each potato so that not one eye
remained—a perfection of paring. And I,
who also often prepared supper for
my father in my mother's absence, power-
fully attached myself to that girl's unsparing
idea of the world, brooking no mistakes, daring
those still alive to rise to her new standard.
Even I couldn't come up to it, lured
though I was by the thought that my goodness
would prevent all evil, even the drunken mess
our family was in: I was about to cry out,
rupturing our world. Tranquilized, I whirled
in a bath of remorse, then curled

in mother's bathrobe, blinking my potato eye
through the haze of a drug she gave me
—my father's Librium—at a loss for what
else to do, since I wept uncontrollably,
begging her to leave my father and save
all our lives, though there we all stayed.
Now baskets of perfect lobelia fly by,
each flower bathrobe blue, with one white eye.
I peel potatoes below, looking out the little
galley window at their blue, untranquilized,
having left that house so long ago. *Now Dear Miss,
you wanted perfection* . . . and found it, whittled
down to a book you couldn't obey. *Be good,*
but leave each potato her imperfect eye,
because something must be left to cry
the tears stored in roots brought out for food.

Housecleaning

Disruption in the bedroom—sheets awry,
uncased pillows, curtains thrown to the blare
of investigating light, nightstand objects
jumbled on the floor near stacked new sheets—why
was the nightstand drawer left open there?
My parents' whole room looked wrecked.

"Hey, what's in there?" Mother's face looked wrecked.
A box of chocolate cherries, lid awry
nested in the opened drawer. "What's in where?"
my mother returned above the panicked blare
of the vacuum cleaner. "Can I have one?" "Why?
You have your own candy," she objected

in perfected, parental reason. "There, there,
it's not so bad," whispered the chocolate objects
rustling their pleats in the darkened lair.
"Another cigarette burn. Now that's wrecked,"
my mother said to the nightstand top, wry
little smile at me. "Give me one, Mom." "Why

can't you have one?" she murmured, "I'll tell you why.
They're mine. They're just for me. There!"
In slamming the drawer she stuck it awry,
jamming the gold cardboard lid. "Objections,
all we've got in this house!" The box was wrecked.
Her pale mouth worked through the glare

of light that passed her chin, desire caught bare
as the stripped mattress we worked to cover. "Why
oh why is the sky so blue," she hummed. Logic wrecked,
hunger says, *Eat*. Empty says, *Sweet*. There, there,
says the unsated hum, though when sated it objects,
How could you? Never eat that again! World awry,

though bedroom straightened. "Put a doily there,
so it won't look wrecked." Drawer straight, light's blare
cut by pulled curtains. Naught awry, even my whine quieted.

The Guilt

Guilt creeps like sheets of insects that erase
bodies down to their skeletons. I can't face
the *Natural History* magazine when insects—
through horrible advances in photography
—are blown up to sticky, gargantuan hairtaffy
and I, the reader, am the haruspex
who knows the future will be cleaned of joy
by the bone-sanding methods guilt employs.

I refused to open up my sister's letters,
overwhelmed with guilt that I had run away
and left her in our parents' house. The orthography
of my name crawled across her floral paper
like fragile, thoracic legs. Unanswered, her letters
came faster, their hoardlike script the raper
of each envelope's field. Was I better
yet? Now should I go back and get her?
The insectile inscribing became an erasing
of what I hoped to be by what I felt I was,
occasionally pictured in science magazines,
something entirely obliterated and picked clean.

Greeting Card Verse

Stop. *Arrêtez.* This message (you're selfish) is:
Go No Further—you won't like it—self-con
slush—a greeting card. Yes! It's fishes
swimming in barbarous iridescence on
a foil background. It's a birthday card (self
is conned) ~~Christmas Mayday~~. Oh dear it's a worth-
day card wishing the receiver (tinfoil self)
had never begun to exist on this earth.
Fishing for a compliment? it says (Turn
page). *Peace on earth,* it says, *WITHOUT YOU.*
Stop. *Arrêtez.* You have to (must!) (*il faut que*) learn
to be invisible. Learn not to exist. (You.)

In the command form, "you" is understood.
Invisible you, never really born.
Ask, *was I ever born?* Was the *would*
I felt ever *will?* No, drift*wood.* Floating
past tinfoil fish. Picture a child forlorn.
Not for long. Get up! Stop being selfish!
(You'll learn when you have children.) The card's a wish.
Like a horizontal, half-parenthesis floating
above the fish, a smile gloats: Merry, merry
un-birthday (it's only childhood trauma)
to you, to you, dressed up as a card. Love, Mama.

The Rule

Completely naked, mons completely gray,
my mother tells me how to masturbate
leaning over the couch where down I lay
in my dream. But I know how! You're too late!
Too often we have to wait for our guides.
Completely naked, mons completely brown,
will I invite her to lie down, who prides
herself on never touching, let alone
holding, stroking, licking? I don't,
though if I wait perhaps she will come of
her own powers, and then we will make love.
Will we be guilty, taking our love loaned
from a dream? Or will curiosity
free us from "Be Still," and let us be?

Upbringing

Bringing yourself up requires long hours alone
to get the nurturing others have felt.
Because of someone else, others have grown up,

so they question why your solitude has grown
so wide, and you wonder at your guilt
that simply being requires these hours alone

with your obstreperous, largely unknown
Being, who only feels and doesn't talk,
whose matted, scaly pelt you've sewn

into what you hope is proper clothing, stock-
still, costumed in a darkness that never melts.
Of course you must take it out when it moans

and let it be naked and chew the bones
and hooves you save for it, after it bolts
around the room and falls, exhausted, down

into the possessed happiness of its selfhood.
This takes hours. As if holding your breath underwater,
you hold in the aboriginal child, attending to the *om*

society seems to breathe that you, a clone,
never seem to understand until you're sick
from something vomiting inside its false home,

and the child feels it's done wrong although
it's only an animal. Now you must clean up alone
or you'll both be sick, or one of you will die.

Of course this takes the hours most spend on the phone,
making money, having kids,
or asking why you don't.

The Job

Seized by fear and anger at my first job
—everybody told me to blow off steam—
I got migraines on weekends, made to rob me
of what everyone called "my fun." Prone, in dream,
drugged by Fiorinal in a darkened room,
I had a kind of respite. When the pain
stretched my skull into a filled balloon,
I fantasized a pink rubber topknot,
a sphincterlike valve to release the blame,
the terror and panic—the steam. I forgot
all about the sphincter, though I'd felt then
it was God's mistake to make us without it,
until I saw a nurse remove a bandage
from what was my mother's clear field of skin
and saw the sphincter reinvented again
as metastasized cancer. Ancient rage,
its outlet abandoned, became molten,
a raw, red pair of lips like a girl's mouth
puffed in terror at having to pretend
she can predict the future and knows the truth
behind the mysterious responsibility
of her new job which she cannot learn
(it is too hard and hurts too much to be
alone and wrong). A ruptured core burns.
Drugged by Haldol in a darkened room,
my mother's job is the job of death.
Grow another mouth. Take another breath.

The Snake

As if all her vertebrae wore tiny
well-designed internal shoes which deftly
writhe as the shoes of commuters writhe
all lined up on a down escalator,
so the thigh-size python stores herself up,
then crawls from the limb's cuff
through her glassed-in world,

                    painted
with a brilliant mural, giving the sense
of false home that murals in offices do—abated,
foreshortened, her screened background the tense
quiver of colors on terminal screens.
Her cage is her office; the zoo is her work.
She performs masterfully her routine
as tenured civil serpent, trained,
restrained.

             But what is her redemption,
if redemption is a being's recognition
of its limits? Hers are mere inches
of the pole she turns around on, her life
an exhibition on bald, denuded branches.
I hope her brain is very large,
her only hope to put a mind in charge,
capacious in imagining her prayer
of what should be there.

I Consider the Possibility

Long-waisted, tender-skinned and, despite the gym,
love roll about the midriff above the leggy limbs
muscled into knots at each calf, "beautiful for your age"
—bend over naked from your waist and show your red half-
peach of cunt to me who has fumbled at my cage
trying key after key in the stuck door with a half-laugh
after each failure; let me lay the bone of my nose
on the peach flesh and lift up my mouth to the pit
as I reach my arms toward the inverted throes
of your breasts, and as I touch your orange nipple tips
know that all my life I've wanted only men
and now, dispossessed of my neglectful mother
who herself toyed with the choice of women,
and upon being merrily teased by my therapist
at the prospect of such a love affair (the male "other"
has never incited such laughter), let me touch your wrist
at the dinner table and begin the silly maneuver
that will lead me to hold your head, to smooth your
hair all back, as in going through keys at the door my wrist
finally turns tender side up as the lock untwists.

The Raptor

Foolishly I'd imagined for you your mother's
death, but now you have your own. At home,
not in a nursing facility, your brother's
cheery, God-filled letters a comfort no one
(well, at least not I) would have predicted,
and me looking in on owlish you, cute
behind big glasses on your tiny head,
the growling, felled pet of your doctors. Acute,
inoperable cancer of the lung, although
you stopped smoking—not soon enough. I wonder
what I'm doing now that will create, under
unknown terms, my own death, far below
the high bright mark of your shadow, entirely
different from you—sharp as an owl's beak in your
awareness, yet drowsy as an owl. Will I
lay rattling the sidebar on my adult crib?
Will you die at home, without a bib,
after years of instructing me
which institution to slot you in?
Who knows what death I'll get exactly,
being daughterless, the line of begetting
neutralized, in hands beyond love.

Yes

What awful thing will I take on
because you've asked? I can't say no.
Too hard to ask? It's only one
more awful thing that I'll take on
and do it all until it's gone,
except the thing will never go.
What awful thing will I take on
because you've asked? I can't say no.

The Gown

After I get mother's gown back on, she starts
to undo tie, then knot, then tie, frantic to get
the gown off, and in the process kicks off
her sheet and blanket. Now her legs are high
in the air, and I'm not looking, I'm covering
again, boosting her up on the bed again,
fixing her sheet before she kicks it off again,
above my birthplace reluctantly hovering,
eyes averted. I've seen it too much,
the gray-haired V of labia closed
around browned minora, poor cheeks scutched up
like a Jersey cow's, tail up, holes exposed.
If only my eyes were like a sculpture's,
smooth, unseeing. Is she without purpose?
Organic brain syndrome, her new diagnosis,
says yes, she really is. But I can't feel sure
she's not insisting she's my baby, my cupcake,
every fifteen minutes until, exhausted, I
realize I can leave. It's a hospital, after all.
I head to the mall.

                    Poppyseed cake and tea.
How shyly some friends have told me
of the glimpses they've had of their parents during
this or that necessary act. But she
is always before my eyes, her endurance,
for me, enduring. Oh stop, stop and die.
Let the body's boundary be inviolable. Let me lie
in bed unafraid to look down, finding yes,
my sex is still my own! I do not look
like her! Let my husband not look
at me and think, as Horace thought of his
old love's vagina, that it looked like a cow's
asshole, wizened and fecal. God how I hate my body,
and you, Horace, over two millennia. But not the way I hate
my mother, my throttled love. Too late,
too late, I'm trespassed now.

Love Beat

How hard I try to kill my love,
its layered substance rank with strength,
appalling in its thickness, knotted as tree roots,
its muscle burled from running from the ax, its length
unmeasurable, for it contracts, footlike,
its tortoise pedal when touched. Its rhubarb stems
and burdock leaves make new love moot,
for my love now is old love, rude-barbed,
a prize vegetable in its prickered bed,
an animal as it thrives.
And the amount of blood that keeps it alive!
I know, for I've spilled it as I've chopped
with my ax at its inscrutable head
and seen its brain regenerate unrobbed,
while its love beat beats unstopped.

Dogged Persistence

Slowly an armchair turns on some sort of pedestal.
Oh Mother I know you will be in it!
I'm here in the fog and vapors, waiting
for you, clear little eyes behind horn-rims,
to look up from your newspaper and stare out
at me, at me! But what a cold look you give.
You do not want to be bothered. *Mom*, I whisper,
it's me. You seem to have a reading lamp
—is that the little glow in the shrouded dimness?
"Don't bother me, Molly." Did you say that?
But I am searching for you! "Leave me alone."
Need, a child's need, a chill airless
panic instead of a mother as your chair
turns its back, and my hands dangle in the cold.
Where are you? You have to be out there somewhere.
I'll find you, I'll find you—how gray the sky is,
the sun a smothered 40-watt bulb behind clouds.
It is snowing, the sky decomposing,
each crystal, as we've all learned, individual,
as each person throughout millennia
is never replicated the same way,
yet out of the millions I will find the one
that is you. I have to.

The Explanation

I won't explain since you can't understand,
nor would I expect you to climb inside
the jewelled crater of my skull and stand
among the ruins, scout among them, then hide

from me, your enemy, inside my own terrain,
crystallized from previous blows—not all yours.
Nor will I now expect you to refrain
from assessment as you stand outdoors,

canvassing my geode skull's smooth surface
and, seeing no clues as to the damage
or to the quirky beauty of old ravage,
urge me again and again to confess

that because I'm hard and hidden from you
you're forced to hysterics from nothing to do.

The Fare

Bury me in my pink pantsuit, you said—and I did.
But I'd never dressed you before! I saw the glint
of gold in your jewelry drawer and popped
the earrings in a plastic bag along with pearls,
a pink-and-gold pin, and your perfume. ("What's this?"
the mortician said . . . "Oh well, we'll spray some on.")
Now your words from the coffin: *Take my earrings off!*
I've had them on all day, for God's sake!
You've had them on five days. The lid's closed,
and the sharp stab of a femininity
you couldn't stand for more than two hours in life
is eternal—you'll never relax. I'm 400 miles away.
Should I call up the funeral home and have them removed?
You're not buried yet—stored till the ground thaws—
where, I didn't ask. Probably the mortician's garage.
I should have buried you in slippers and a bathrobe.
Instead, I gave them your shoes. Oh, please
do it for me. I can't stand the thought of you
pained by vanity forever. Reach your cold hand
up to your ear and pull and hear the click
of the clasp hinge unclasping, then reach
across your face and get the other one
and—this effort could take you days, I know,
since you're dead. Let it be your last effort:
to change my mistake and be dead in comfort.
Lower your hands in their places

on your low mound of stomach and rest, rest,
you can let go. They'll fall
to the bottom of the casket like tokens,
return fare fallen to the pit
of a coat's satin pocket.

Miss, Miss, Are You Awake?

What real flowers are these fake ones made to be?
Floppy peach heads, rapt on green wires, reach up
to the customers who slide into the booth
(gray leatherette, slow waitress, tea in a pot).
To love their copy natures is to love
by remembering what has come down to you
—for whatever it came *from* is long gone.
They are the embalmed versions, the mummies,
swaddled in cloth by painstaking hands
who reconstruct each stamen, leafbol, pistil,
like morticians. My mother loved them.
"Doesn't she look beautiful?" her friends said
as they slid by to stare at her coffin,
the same as they'd say in a tearoom like this,
"Doesn't it look beautiful?" As I stopped here
on my way to the hospital, from the hospital,
to the apartment, from the empty apartment,
three hours each way through snow, I stopped
being repelled by cheap imitation,
understanding it's what I have, like
the lipsticked corpse that didn't really look
like her. Now I look at the flowers' faces,
unable to identify them either, and find
a welcome in their plumped satin centers
like the quilted satin in coffins. Before
the slow, slow waitress comes, I climb in.
Until I place my order I'm wrapped on their stem.

another
love

Religious Instruction

No fires are built (except spiritual ones)
in the rectory fireplace, full of philodendrons
which stare directly out at the orphans

(grown-up ones) seated in front of them. Father
sits to one side with Bonnie the dog super-
vising the group of two whose spirits stir

slowly. It's cold in here: stewed tea, winter rain,
sweaters, prayer books, questions almost restrained,
then asked awkwardly, revealing a naked moraine

of bald rocks and dirt left by glaciers receding
somewhere in these two women alternately reading
the Creed aloud, in their mourning needing

(Bonnie yawns, but the priest, amused and stern,
a widower himself, insists that they learn
to walk the scaffolds of the Trinity to mourn

what smashed so far below) . . . needing what?
A Heavenly Parent now that the real ones are gone. Cut
like paper dolls from the tall city's book, they've shut,

with effort, the heavy rectory door to sit with a priest
and his dog in the dead of winter where at least
a fire might be lit in the fireplace for Christ's

sake. Instead the hearth is filled with greens,
a houseplant arrangement in homely baskets: green
fire. Father explains what everything means.

But what *does* everything mean? The collie yawns,
mouth wide open, her foul breath a wind that spawns
migrations across imaginary lawns

—green fire—to the other side, into God's mirth.
Can these three orphans laugh on earth?
Dog thumps tail on hearth.

Can they take themselves lightly?
What can the rough stone rectory rectify?
Less than weighs on them nightly.

How pleasant, now that they are man and women, to obey,
saying what they were taught to say
now that the work week is over, and it's Saturday

when thought roams in daydream, which is thought's right,
ranging, leash dangling, for the ritual words unknot
what was tied, and what was intolerable is not.

In a Long Line of Horses

Sweet tang of horse at dry edge of canyon,
steep tiny path descends, as subway stairs
descend through platforms in complex stations.
Clumsy, citified, never ridden a mare,
never been to a canyon of deep urban architecture
unearthed by celestial hands and turned to light,
man-made become god-made. God's maid I am,
thrilled to look agoraphobically down to the right:
drop to death immediate. "Don't lean, ma'am,"
the cowboy says. I straighten, of course,
and think with sudden pleasure of the animal below,
scratch her ears, and talk to her, though all
she loves is her chapped angel, the cowboy.
They lead hundreds into the canyon. We each enjoy
a superficial blue moment on her back. As pilgrims
we are not individuals in control. Her whim
to throw us may be her inner call. To trust
that she will do her work is our work
as we follow the stations of the canyon thrust
into our saddles against good city reason.
Where is the train? We are the train.

Subway Vespers

Thank you for some ventilation and a pole for my hands.
Thank you that the man with whiskey breath and
bloodshot eyes, business suit, plus monogrammed

cuffs (likely to behave) is significantly
taller than I am, leaving me inches of free
space between my place at the pole, his, and the lady

weeping below me. Over the loudspeaker a voice
informs us a track obstruction leaves no choice
but for a man to check each car's wheels twice.

Obstruction? Must be a body. Try to see:
nothing but black tunnel walls and the guilty
heads of those with seats. Thank you for my dusty clothes,

and that we are not naked in a cattle car.
After they find the body, we won't have to walk far.
A man's legs dangle above the door ...

but he's alive, mumbling into his beeper.
The conductor replies on the loudspeaker,
"Only garbage on the track!" You, our keeper,

we thank you for releasing the brake.
We'll go home, buyers of fish, bread, and steak,
to sit and watch the news we do not make.

The engine starts. My prayer implodes with a red
shot of relief that we won't be led
down a tunnel, past a corpse, out from the track bed,
but delivered to a lighted station instead.

Simple

When the wafer dissolves on my tongue I won-
der what part of the Lord I have eaten,
His scrotum molecularly recon-
structed in a pale disc, or a wheaten
flap of armpit? Perhaps internal organs
vaporized to universal atoms
from the thorax of our Lord. Others had plans
to preserve the saints in bits, the phantom
of Anthony's larynx in a ruby vase,
Agatha's breasts in gold caskets, the flesh
reserved. I only eat our Lord and mas-
ticate the host, the church a crèche,
and I in my stall not even knowing how
to blow glass housing for a saint or wield
a hammer with my hoof, unable to bow
or scoop breasts into a box. The world
transubstantiates me to animal
evolving in reverse: soon I could be a lizard
on the wall of the manger, in time one-celled,
perhaps a single cell of the baby Lord,
perhaps His tongue, so what I chew as symbol
I might at last become: simple.

Forgiveness

Forgiveness is not an abstraction for
it needs a body to feel its relief.
Knees, shoulders, spine are required to adore
the lightness of a burden removed. Grief,
like a journey over water completed,
slides its keel in the packed sand reef.
Forgiveness is contact with the belief
that your only life must now be lived. Knees
once sank into the leather of the pew with all
the weight of created hell, of whom you did not ease,
or what you did not seize. Now the shortfall
that crippled your posture finds sudden peace
in the muscular, physical brightness
of a day alive: the felt lightness
of existence self-created, forgiveness.

No

Nothing grows a callus without a rub,
the constant irritation, then the raw,
red, leaking blister in response. The Law
of Skin is: eventual callus. Now scrub
any stain on the world with your hands!
While the callous response seems unfeeling,
it's only that the feeling
is done. And out of your hands.

Unseen

Behind this bamboo screen in my underwear
I watch my friend feed her parrots on the porch,
this and a floppy canvas shade our only wall,

about the thickness of a mainsail. Here
two dogs and a handyman join her, while I eat lunch
in a solitude as naked as a bathroom stall.

From this planned, reciprocal ignorance
she makes a kindness more intense than touch,
since it is actual touch withheld.

I am a sea she lowers her shade to, much
as she loves a vista, and in the new innocence
she leaves me to, feel closely held.

She's even got the dogs not to bother me,
and the birds mute in their makeshift tree.

Floral Conversation

Bursting with news—which friend to tell it to?
Neurotic, exciting, and morally
questionable—the one you choose will have to
tolerate you in a bad light. Corollary?
Pick one who loves ambiguity. Choosing
her hands and face, like petal and leaf, the skin
to photosynthesize your news, refusing
the shadow you cast yourself in, kin
to your enthusiasms, like a blue
delphinium next to a speckled foxglove
whispering in the garden, is what you
are bursting to find: someone to love
for liking you. As with two in the midday garden,
one might shade the other from the glare,
altering your light by her presence there.

Vogue Vista

Since each old scar on my face seems a stone pillar
sunk below now tiered and gardened gradations,
discovering that caves of ruins were filler
in the making of this villa's new foundations
seems a natural progression toward this elegant
fête where you, my former love, my ex-founder, are bent
toward the opalescent skin below the eyes
of a Roman beauty. Your self-satisfied
sound of expansion to her flutter-laughter jars
the settings down the long table to where I am seated
between bored merchants. What I feel makes me
despair of what I feel: she is of god. Depleted
in my own planned vista, hurt and angry,
I am so human all I make is from a dying world.
You are a child in her goddess arms twirled.
Her face is a caper furled in its flower.
My hands fly batlike to my scars.

Portrayal

Hearing about a friend's friend over years,
not meeting that person perhaps for years,
then only at a social occasion
where both of you awkwardly need to shun
the intimacies you've near-feasted on,
is like the view from still lifes hung
on opposite sides of a gallery wall:
she the rabbit carcass strung upside down,
surrounded by cherries, lemons, and bowls;
you the trout splayed on blue-and-white towels
with grapes and eggs. Both of you are painted
by your friend's art, your connection created
by your own secrets inside the framed
flay which resembles you, beside her name.

Baubles After Bombs

Little metal symbols gambol in the bright
pastures of the cases—the world in sight
for a moment, coincidences hinged
together in a genuine plan, parts phalanged
as finger joints, clasped and ringed
in the jewelry display. Elsewhere someone's job
is picking arms and fingers from war rubble,
while we pick out our pins, one a cat's head—
it doesn't look severed at all. Meant to be
displayed with turquoise eyes that do not sob,
chin a perfect end to its body . . . Rubble
searching for human debris is all our job, bent
on recovering as we are, so in this case we see
our hopes made gold facts. Beauty in a world sacked
is whimsy's rearrangement of organs and limbs,
all things in miniature akin: a frog's head,
a dog's head, gemmed hearts chained to a pin.

The Hunt

The stubby black-jowled dog inside me growls
and drools and warns and plants its crooked feet,
legs quivering, brindle chest staunched, and howls
until approachers back off in defeat,
although a brilliant poacher sometimes cows
my dog, my heart, its bitten hope, with meat,
flung viscera my tamed dog mauls
and then protects, well guarding what I eat
while poacher raises rifle: he follows
my deer into my wood, calling me dear, fleet
beauty, and I run, wholly my wild soul,
while the dumb, bristled dog I too am prowls,
guarding empty gate and empty street
till hunter becomes me, and we repeat.

Interrupted Elegy

Draw a bath without bubbles. Warm water
with a slightly yellowish cast. (Imagine
life as a window to itself.) No food for
two days before—all evacuated. Sin
to let a big mess spoil it. (Your bowels go
into spasm when you die.) Step in. Put
your head back on the ledge. Place the blade so
it's easily reached. When relaxed and warm, cut
across each wrist beneath the water's skin
and let blood flow like the ancient Romans.
But doesn't a bath defy self-denial?
Clear, but unlike glass, it laps. Nothing
can be cut from it. There is your frail
body in the tub's womb, where you feel pain
my darling thing, because you feel warm.

Happy Birthday

Whenever I feel I am most myself,
a baking cake welled up beyond its pan
is what I am, anchored, yet uncontained. The gulf
I feel whenever I am most myself
between my sides and insides on the oven shelf
overflowing, like words outpouring, not by plan,
is itself the me I am when I am most myself:
a cake out loud! its mouth the pan.

Instructions to Miss Muffet

Your costume for Halloween is "Miss Muffet
Revisited." Please come to the party
with your own curds, whey, and tuffet.
Sit in the midst of ghosts with warty
rubber masks, beatifically eating
cottage cheese, your blue dress plumped satinly
about this tuffeted footstool. Defeating
spiders, once so hard, will be your specialty.
The hairy manylegs that made you quiver
at what you thought were reminders
of webby mental horrors will not be real
after you examine them, creeping back
to the tuffet to retrieve your broken bowl
after you've been frightened away. You lack
courage—or maybe only *age* to add
to *coeur*—which time achieves. You'll see,
it's only the last legs of fear, all in a sad
mess of cottage cheese, nothing that would lure
you, entrap you, destroy you. Going back
for the rest of your whey will restore you.
You have to eat to live, you aren't fantasy,
though you'll appear so at this party, back
where you began, amidst embodied ghouls.
But now you have a new dress and a new bowl.

Goodbye Hello in the East Village

Three tables dow[n] .... Ginsberg we sit
in JJ's Russian .... ‑iend,
who's strugg[l]
on knowin[g]
to my tro[u] .... if I
didn't know y
faking this good cru
bright openings like a h[u] .... s fur.
(My friend is half an orphan. .... in here.)
The East Village shuffles past JJ's window,
and we hear Allen order loudly in the ear
of the waitress, *"Steamed only! No cholesterol!"*
"I could tell you it's my marriage, Nita,
and how much I love my new life in two countries,
but the real reason," I beam irresistibly at a
dog walker with 8 dogs on leashes in the freezing
evening outside JJ's window where we sit,
"is that I'm *an orphan. It's over.* They're
both dead." Her lids narrow her eyes to a slit
of half-recognition. "I couldn't say this,"—there!
the waitress plunks two bowls of brilliant magenta
borscht, pierogi, and hunks of challah
—"to just *anybody,*"—jewel heaps of food on Formica
—only to you, who wouldn't censure me,
since you've witnessed me actually fantasize
chopping their heads from their necks from their limbs

to make a soup of the now dead Them to feed
the newly happily alive Me.

                              An old order is dimmed,
just as now the U.S., its old enemy
the USSR vaporized, disarms itself,
nearly wondering what a century's fuss
was all about . . . what *was* my fuss about? (The wealth
of relief after decades of distrust,
makes you wonder why you did it, until
you remind yourself of how it was.)
But even a struggle to the death is levelled
in the afterlife of relief. A bevel
in the glass of America has connected
along a strip of this life to the window
of JJ's restaurant connecting Nita and me, wed
to the nightlife on Second Avenue, though
in reflection only, the reflection that now perfectly
joins Ginsberg with his steamed vegetables
and us with our steamy borscht and pierogi
to the ice-pocked sidewalk, God's table,
full of passersby, pointing occasionally to Allen,
joined now by an Asian boy, but more often
just hurrying past in the cold as we eat
the food of a previous enemy
and find it brightly delicious—*it is meet*

and right so to do—in the world now ours,
the century's hours hurtling behind
like snow-wake off an empty dogsled.
Old friends, we rest, not talking, well fed,
since at this cold dark moment things are fine.

Matins

Rain hisses off the bus and car and taxi tires,
hosing the almost gardened streets; blackened lanes
of traffic seem planned as garden paths;
buildings wired like cemented topiaries
lean into their baths, and it's spring,
we're alive, the city a human-made Eden,
so gray, not green, though there in the fruit stands
jonquils and hyacinths bow in tin buckets and
figures in slickers duck out to shop, a wet parade
of flower heads conveyed along below.
It occurs to me to pray.
In a little seizure, a prayer shudders up,
its spasm quick as a camera's shutter:
Glad you exist to rise up, window.

All Her Life That Bra Strap

All her life that bra strap slipped off her left
shoulder—to be jacked up surreptitiously.
All her life burnt barren plainness left
her so hopeless that frivolity
grew essential to her. And still all
her years she worried how others judged her
—the expense of charm! (Not that this stopped her.
The hanging bra strap: periwinkle satin.) All
her childhood she hated roads; they couldn't talk.
She loved the round: marbles; globes with continents
and oceans that gravity pulled inward. Balked
by flatness (highway, noon, chicken wire fence),
her life drained out of her, restored only
by the circles of converging city streets,
multipaned as insect eyes, or well-cut gems, or Keats,
who could talk. Found comfort. How plain was lonely.
How round, how fibered and sound: her breasts in
their lace nests. Nipples, cat's-eye marbles,
the cat's real eyes in its round fur face. In-
to, into, into a deep center somewhere, bless
the luxury of manifold texture.
The soft loop of the strap halfway down her
upper arm all her life like an arm around her,
a voice to protect her, like Keats's murmur.

Prairie Prayer

Time rolls out like a prairie.
Do not be afraid.
The mind forms a prayer
from endless land's creed.

The straight-blade horizon
is grass blades in billions,
silver slanted in the sun,
the prairie soft bullion

beyond stamp or use,
unowned, undone, unformed.
A prayer forms alone
when time undoes, unforms.

The self, like land itself,
beyond stamp or use
in its unfarmed wealth,
telescopes into the mind.

Now, if the mind had fingers
it would touch its thought.
Such contact would be prayer,
an endless plain inside there.